CIVIL SOCIETY
and the

Zuma
GOVERNMENT

OPPORTUNITIES for ENGAGEMENT

Edited by Yvette Geyer and Ivor Jenkins

2009

Idasa would like to extend our thanks to the funders of this project, the International Development Research Centre (IDRC), for supporting this dialogue and making this publication possible.

idasa
AN AFRICAN DEMOCRACY INSTITUTE

ISBN 978-1-920409-10-4

First published 2009

Editing by *Hilda Hermann, Purple Comma*
Design and cover design by *Orchard Publishing*
Bound and printed by *Top Copy, Cape Town*

Contents

Civil Society and the Zuma Administration in South Africa

YVETTE GEYER
Portfolio and Project Development Facilitator

Background

OVER THE PAST DECADE, THE STATE OF CIVIL SOCIETY AROUND THE GLOBE has been an issue of discourse among development practitioners. The role and function of civil society has sometimes been called anything from a 'magic bullet' for solving development challenges, through to being accused of being as the lackeys of the Washington Consensus. This project aimed to host a round table focused on understanding the potential opportunities and challenges that South African civil society can expect in building democracy into the fifth democratic administration as part of a broader interrogation of the role of civil society. In addition, it was hoped that the round table would assist in identifying future areas of work for civil society in relation to political action.

In order to lay the foundation for discussion, three research papers were commissioned. The round-table conversation was held in Pretoria at the Idasa Kutlwanong Democracy Centre on 21 August 2009.

Primary themes

The key areas that Idasa and its partner, the International Development Research Centre (IDRC), were interested in exploring included:

- What is the role of civil society?
- What are the areas of involvement for civil society?
- Are there policy recommendations to be made?
- What areas of research need to be explored?

Role of civil society

Divergent perspectives were raised by the speakers regarding the role of civil society in the South African context. Much is often made of the role that was played by civil society in the transition to democracy and a perspective tabled indicated that, by organising through a common movement, civil society played an important historical role. This perspective was challenged through a position which suggested that perhaps civil society in its truest form did not exist prior to 1994, but was rather an attempt to recreate a State that was not serving the majority of the populace. It is important to distinguish between the different roles of civil society prior to 1994, with some organisations directly providing service delivery, others engaging in social welfare support, and others agitating for political change.

Post-transition, several dynamics have impacted on the role and effectiveness of civil society. It was highlighted that a loss of leadership to the newly emerging democratic State had a significant influence on the role of civil society and its ability to impact on government programmes.

It appears that there is limited space for critique of developments in the country without fear of intimidation. This state of play is, however, not only referring to the State, but also includes intra-civil society discourse and engagement. It was contended that in many instances the African National Congress (ANC) as the dominant political force in the country uses civil society organisations (CSOs) in a cynical way to further its political objectives.

This could be further compounded by a shallow level of civil society in South Africa that speaks for a limited section of the population. This reality is physically manifested by protests throughout the country and across many sectors of development. In essence, civil society remains in the making, particularly at community level. It is often the case that, where there is a call for involvement, the outcome is tension rather than resolution of the developmental challenges. There is a clear trend that people's patience in waiting for meaningful change is on the wane. Debates on this issue are starting to take place in different parts of the country. Three views from round tables interrogating civil society that were hosted by the University of Johannesburg have identified the following perspectives:

- There are undemocratic forces at play.
- Democracy cannot be consolidated if power remains within parties.
- That the majority party lost votes across most provinces presents an opportunity for democratic diversity.

Is there emerging consensus that the idea of 'service delivery' is inherently undemocratic? If so, what are the appropriate levels of democracy in relation to development imperatives?

Involvement of civil society

Perhaps the most critical point that emerged from the discussion is that civil society has an influence on the whole of society, not just government, although that has traditionally been the point of focus. It is necessary to become more strategic about the interface with government and building social alliances.

The Zuma administration seems to be more open and there is potentially an opportunity for healthy expression, particularly with regard to practical projects that can be undertaken jointly between civil society and government. The newly set up clustered ministries also present myriad opportunities for influence. In addition, the planning process of the new government is a potential point of entry for advocacy with which civil society needs to engage.

Both fluidity in the ruling party and space for influence were highlighted. ANC members complain about their lack of influence as the South African Communist Party (SACP) and the Congress of South African Trade

Unions (COSATU) – as CSOs – have better access to ANC policy, which minimises the influence of party members. In seeking to understand its impact on society as a whole, and government specifically, civil society needs to consider gender, current global circumstances and, above all, the need to guard its independence.

Areas for further exploration

South African civil society specifically needs to clarify opportunities, the imperatives to act on as a movement, and to interface with constitutional democracy as a concept. The gaps that are currently not being addressed by civil society include *inter alia*, the National Prosecuting Authority (NPA) and the identification of core strategic issues that should be focused on by civil society as a whole.

The need for further research

The research that exists on South African civil society is paltry in nature and needs to be invested in – not only in terms of longitudinal understanding, but also in terms of depth. Potential points of interest to be unpacked through further research include:

- The diversity of civil society in South Africa.
- Clarifying the assumption and often-stated notion that democratic process can be an obstacle to development.
- Is civil society itself democratic?
- The independence of civil society vs. the participation of civil society in building a nation.

Attendees

Forty-two people attended the workshops – 21 men and 22 women – representing four sectors: two from academia, 34 from South African CSOs, five from international CSOs and two from government (one South African and one international).

Conclusion

The participants expressed gratitude for the opportunity to reflect and discuss the role of their work and what it means within a broader context. It has prompted many thoughts for further consideration in the work they do as daily development practitioners.

New World Governance and the Emergence of a Global Community Round Table

The Role of Civil Society in the New Administration

Raenette Taljaard
Independent analyst and consultant

ANY DISCUSSION OF THE ROLE OF CIVIL SOCIETY IN PROTECTING AND promoting South African democracy has to start with the significant contribution South African civil society, in all its various incarnations, has played in the realisation of the very democracy in which it seeks to play different and more nuanced roles today. This includes areas as varied as strengthening the parliamentary oversight of the new administration and new structures of governance and government, and the involvement of civil society in tracking the ability of government to realise a better life for all South Africans in terms of service delivery.

Even a cursory glance at South Africa's contemporary history during the 1980s will bear testimony to the fact that it was trade union movements, United Democratic Front (UDF) structures and organised civil society that contributed in significant measure to the changes that were brought about. The important continuity challenge that arises is to ensure that civil society plays a role in engaging civic action that is positive in nature, even where protest actions are concerned, and does not become counterproductive as a mirror-image of civil disobedience campaigns that hallmarked a completely different era in completely different circumstances. The waves of violent protest action and what has been termed 'service delivery unrest' pose a significant challenge to both government and civil society organisations (CSOs) to deepen South African democracy substantively, in order to ensure that people feel that they have a voice. This voice needs to be proactively channelled into positive change for long-term social stability.

Herein lies the crux of the challenge for all parties in South Africa: to deepen democracy. There can be very little doubt that the global slowdown and local recession is placing enormous pressure on South Africa's unequal, class- and race-stratified social fabric. The democratically elected government is now in its fourth term of office, 15 years after the advent of democracy. This has coincided with global circumstances that have sharply and starkly highlighted the immense task we continue to face to bring about meaningful change to a formerly socially engineered society that still bears the scars of its past while it slowly seeks to undo its devastating consequences for the majority of its people. There can be very little doubt – as was seen in the flare-ups, strikes and social unrest during the new president's first 100 days in office – that people's patience is waning and that the pressure on government to reach deep into their material living conditions with meaningful steps has increased exponentially over its four terms of office.

The new administration has clearly spelt out that its core objective will be social change and that it will make all efforts to secure the better future electoral victory promise as its core mandate. Key appointments have been made and governance structures reformed in order to facilitate this objective being realised. It is therefore significant to note that it is not only in the tone of the new administration that a great deal of promise is present for a new role for CSOs, but also in the structure of government. This includes the creation of a National Planning Commission (NPC), the release of a Medium Term Strategic Framework (MTSF) and a plethora of new ministries and complex debates about the economic growth path

South Africa should follow in a completely altered global economic landscape, to what strategic alliances ought to be formed in foreign policy, to what social security models would be best suited to secure social stability in a complex and unequal society. These debates are the lifeblood of South Africa's efforts to secure a meaningful freedom dividend for its people, and the new administration has clearly indicated that these debates must be as inclusive as possible, heralding a promising new chapter in civil society/government relations.

The core challenge for civil society is complex. It saw a significant number of its leaders drawn into government as apartheid ended and liberation came. This trend has continued to an extent and complex questions have arisen over time about the role of civil society and strategic imperatives. Historically, civil society was a key component of the liberation struggle and it had to redefine its role in relation to government. During the Mbeki era, this redefinition was often painful as civil society sought to grapple with playing a role in forging ahead on accountability and governance issues, while often having its motives questioned by government. What has been of particular interest is the extent to which the new administration, at least in principle, appears to welcome a role for civil society as a multiplier of the oversight and accountability framework. However, only time will answer whether this is definitively the case or whether some remnants of the suspicion of the motives of civil society organs remain.

South African civil society has a three-fold role to play. It must contribute to policy discourse as the country grapples with much slower economic growth and responses, shifts in global fiscal and monetary policies, clean energy and climate change, and human capital formation through social investment. It must continue to play a watchdog and oversight role, assisting parliament and, ultimately, government, by being the eyes and ears of the people. It must be present on the ground at grassroots level to ensure that the crucial feedback loop that is often missing in public life in the context of a dysfunctional electoral system continues to ensure that policy and practise are closely aligned in pursuit of meaningful change. All these roles are crucial and different organs of civil society will have different responsibilities to which they are particularly suited.

The new administration has opened up a host of new possibilities – in style, substance and form – for civil society to play new and meaningful roles in shaping policy discourse and the direction of debates on service delivery, and the realisation of a better life for all in the context of the global financial meltdown and its local recession consequences that have limited the scope for government action to ameliorate poverty and deprivation. The presence of the new administration has done this in at least three meaningful ways:

First, the prevailing political culture of perfunctory and cursory attention to inputs by civil society has been replaced by a seemingly more open and accommodating leadership and political culture that has welcomed debate, discussion and dissent as healthy expressions in a democratic State. This is a refreshing change from the prevalent political culture of the Mbeki years, which frequently viewed and labelled such dialogue, debate and dissent as unpatriotic or problematic. Although the new administration is still in its early stages, the initial signals of a different political culture in which civil society can broadly make its contributions must be welcomed.

Second, significant restructuring and redesign of government has meant that various policy spaces have been opened up again to debate and discussion, and a sense of partnership or fostering partnerships appears to be in the offing. While more can always arguably be done in the context of the global slowdown and its local effects, the manner in which government has engaged civil society, even prior to the 2009 elections, to craft a framework agreement to address the crisis, and the efforts that have been made to build a partnership between business, labour and government to create a skills retraining fund for workers who may lose their jobs, has demonstrated a real willingness to do business differently. These consultations open up significant opportunities for civil society. The fact that government has created a new set of clustered ministries has multiplied the opportunities open to CSOs to contest spaces and policies in new forms and with new arguments in new contexts. The same is evident with respect to foreign policy, where certain shifts and interactions have taken place. These are, in part, due to civil society lobbying on key questions such as South Africa's stance on Sudan and Omar al-Bashir. The same can be said about Burma (Myanmar), another topic of significant civil society contestation.

Third, the emergence of new political parties and players, and the slow but steady realignment of South African politics towards a more issue-based than identity-driven public policy space, while still in its infancy, holds longer-term promise for civil society actions and interactions around issue-based politics and polity. In this regard, the fourth democratically elected parliament is brimful with new members and committee structures that have been crafted to mirror the structural changes in government. All of these structures will create new opportunities for interaction between elected representatives and civil society.

While the new administration confronts new challenges, so too must civil society. The new administration appears willing to take civil society contributions on board and, on key issues, civil society will have to forge a much better form of internal cooperation and coherence to maximise the opportunities it has to have its voice heard. Civil society needs to reassess the mode and manner in which it wishes to capitalise on these new opportunities to interact with government and to simultaneously guard its independence. Given its history and the manner in which civil society has had to adapt to constantly changing circumstances in South Africa's body politic – significant historical and political shifts that have posed challenges for role definition – the advent of a new administration may well have heralded a new challenge of balancing partnership and independence in pursuit of policy contributions, oversight roles and grassroots roles, all of which enhance the overall quality of democracy through various interactions with the State at different levels.

South African civil society has traditionally used an array of devices: lobbying parliament, quiet interactions with the executive, court actions and litigation, and partnerships with various Chapter Nine bodies. All of these avenues will continue to be used, but the nature of possible civil society/government interactions and partnerships will pose new and interesting challenges.

There is one such challenge, amidst myriad others, that requires emphasis: the question of gender. It will be particularly crucial to address gender issues specifically to ensure that the gains that have been made – evidenced in a significant number of women in government and some boardrooms – do not obscure the ongoing challenges women face. This is not an either/or debate; their presence in elected structures and executive bodies is as important as their broader voice in dealing with questions of poverty, marginalisation and violence that remain all too often the real face of South Africa's women in a male-dominated society.

There have been various lapses in this regard: recent statistics on female representation on boards and at executive management level has shown small declines. An unfortunate all-male Cabinet composition and the furore over female representation at the executive level of government in the Western Cape, as well as sexist comments by opposition politicians in the Western Cape Provincial Legislature are out of synch with a society that prizes its women. Resurgent debates about the role of women continues to surprise those who believed that many of these questions were definitively settled with the equality and affirmative action clauses in the Constitution.

Furthermore, the complications that arise in the context of gender were appropriately highlighted by former parliamentary speaker – and South Africa's first female speaker – Dr Frene Ginwala, who used an address at the University of Johannesburg to fire a necessary and apposite broadside at the fact that the establishment of a women's ministry, lumped together with children and the disabled, has effectively disguised the ongoing male domination of South Africa. These issues are very real and defensive debates cannot obscure that South African civil society will have a special role to play in ensuring that gender issues and the persistent violence against women that plagues our society remain at the forefront of concerns if we are to build a stable society. The ministry's response that all three of these 'groups' will receive equal attention completely misses the mark of the conceptual questions Dr Ginwala raised, and adds to the concerns of various gender-related CSOs that welcomed her comments.

South African civil society has a long and proud history of being an active role-player in the birth-pangs of democracy. While it has gone through various processes of self-critique and self-definition, its value in playing a crucial role in evolving debates about the kind of society South Africa forges out of the ashes of social engineering, and the nature of democracy built under the banner of the Constitution, will remain a beacon to those who seek real and substantive change. Defining the tone, methods and modalities of how best to do this in a new era of engagement with a new administration, new structures and a different prevailing wind of a political culture of tolerance, thus far in its early days, at least, will be key.

Thoughts on the State of Civil Society in South Africa

KHEHLA SHUBANE
Research Associate
Centre for Policy Studies

CIVIL SOCIETY HAS BEEN CREDITED WITH A CONSIDERABLE ROLE IN facilitating the end of apartheid. Without the militant strikes, a variety of boycotts and generalised political mobilisation, which became a defining feature of State-social relations years before the end of apartheid, the political changes that saw the introduction of democracy in South Africa could not have been possible. Through various actions, civil society made it impossible for apartheid to continue. By effectively mobilising communities against the State and its ideology, civil society withdrew the cooperation of the governed from being governed by apartheid, thus outflanking the considerable might of government that could be brought to bear on communities that were unarmed. The might of the State was not used as it was not suited to securing the consent of the oppressed in the continued existence of apartheid.

The laudatory theme towards civil society suddenly changed once democracy had been achieved. It was argued that, in the immediate aftermath of the first democratic elections, civil society was immobilised. Many groups that had been part of civil society appeared so enamoured of the new order that they felt the democracy they had striven for would be guaranteed by groups with whom they had shared visions of a democratic new order to supplant apartheid. Civic associations, youth, women and even trade union formations, which were a key feature of many localities in the country, went into a sharp decline. The United Democratic Front (UDF), an organisation that coordinated the various struggles of these groups, decided to dissolve itself and encourage members of its affiliates to join the African National Congress (ANC). Many members of affiliate organisations had, in any case, already joined the ANC when it was unbanned and provided the basis for building branches across the country.

The dissolution of the UDF suggested to those who had fought against apartheid that their role in civil society was no longer required. Having fought for so long and hard, the ANC could not possibly constitute a threat to democracy that would require the continued existence of civil society organisations (CSOs) to ensure democracy was expanded under an ANC-led government.

As soon as it was unbanned, the ANC became the most powerful popular organisation. This should have raised questions about the role of CSOs in ensuring power was indeed used to enhance democracy. Civic associations, which had led many boycotts in many communities, became moribund, and in their place ANC branches emerged that could not draw in as many members as the civics they were supplanting. Partly this was a result of the partisan nature of the ANC. Some who had been members of civics held political views that were in competition with those of the ANC. In the immediate aftermath of the unbanning of the ANC, trade unions too seemed to have been crippled by the loss of an experienced layer of leadership. These leaders moved on to play other roles, especially in the ANC, and later in government and business. This fate also befell many other popular organisations.

Of the many CSOs of the past, the trade union movement reorganised and regained its mass-based power. It soon grew to eclipse the ANC in terms of number of members once the latter became a governing party and faced the challenges of governing. Other groups that formed part of civil society were unable to reorganise themselves; various attempts at rekindling some of them failed. The Soweto Electricity Crisis Committee might have been an attempt to recreate the Soweto Civic Association or the Soweto Parents Crisis Committee, but the organisation was unable to rise up and gain the broad appeal that these organisations had been able to garner.

The youth, many of whom had been members of the South African Youth Congress (SAYCO), and women, who were part of Federation of South African Women (FSAW), were channelled into the Youth and Women's Leagues of the ANC.

The Youth League became very active in ANC affairs, but the Women's League in effect became moribund – only coming to life during elective conferences, making occasional statements, and hosting rallies or meetings during a few days commemorating one or other occasion related to women. As an organisational force it is totally ineffective.

The South African Communist Party (SACP), an old party that had functioned in an alliance with the ANC, retained its identity and strengthened itself into an elite party of relatively few individuals. This was by choice as the SACP believes it should retain its status as a party of what it views as politically advanced individuals. This has not stopped the party playing a role well in excess of the number of its members. Again, this is in line with a deliberate policy. It operates closely with the trade union federation, which it views and nurtures as the mass organisation of the people whom it would like to enlist into its ranks once satisfied they have reached the right level of political maturity to become communists.

Civil society dynamics

South Africa undoubtedly has a reasonably well-established civil society track record; several non-State groups have existed to advance myriad causes, both connected to the business of the State and not. In their functioning, these groups have undoubtedly improved the quality of democracy in the country. Many have, consciously or not, served to diversify points at which power can be exercised. Some of them play so useful a role that they receive direct State support, which goes beyond merely reinforcing the existence of a law-governed environment in which to advance their objectives.

To the extent that the chief business of civil society is to expand democracy by affording individuals who are part of these formations space to express their views, South Africa is well endowed with such groups. Many of these exist to consciously expand their power relative to government.

Thus, they self-consciously seek to diversify formal power located within government. By establishing the fact that power can be diversified not just to other tiers of government or special entities created and controlled by government, these CSOs have extended the space for democratic expression to civil society groups that lack an overt political identity to be accepted as role-players in the life of society.

In the past, civil society was distorted by the overbearing nature of apartheid. This policy conditioned responses of the entire society to the extent that groups that would otherwise not have had a political identity/role were forced to take a stand against it. This was a distortion of civil society in that it over-politicised groups whose objective it was to address myriad issues that did not seek to focus directly on political questions. The imposition of racial division on civil society meant that groups that served blacks tended to be political. Whatever their objectives, they were under pressure to take a stand against apartheid.

In contrast, groups serving whites engaged in a manner that approximated the role of civil society relative to the State. Members of such groups could use democratic means to bring their influence to bear on the State. They were free to argue with policymakers for laws to be changed. In a limited way, relations between groups representing whites and the State were normal and susceptible to democratic influence in a way that was not possible for groups representing blacks.

In a manner somehow not too dissimilar, current civil society suffers distortions that make it difficult for it to be regarded as such without any problems. Few CSOs in present-day South Africa have amassed considerable power that they can employ to dominate the realm in which other CSOs exist. The SACP,[1] the Congress of South African Trade Unions (COSATU) and the Youth League – organisations that have a very close relationship with the governing party – dominate civil society in an entirely unhealthy manner. Both COSATU and the SACP are in a formal alliance with the ANC, and the Youth League is an ANC subsidiary organisation. The former two hold rather elaborate viewpoints based on their values, which they use as a basis for grappling with policy issues. They are very clear that their viewpoints are a matter for their members to alter

1   Gevisser, M. 2007. *Thabo Mbeki: The Dream Deferred* Jonathan Ball Publishers, Johannesburg, pp 467-468

and no one else. This stance has never prevented them from altering ANC policies if they differ with them.

In contrast, the Youth League espouses no ideological viewpoint that has been shared with the public, but effectively operates as if it were a subsidiary of both COSATU and the SACP. It appears to take its cue from these organisations. It has occasionally expressed differences with the ANC and aligned itself in contentious issues with COSATU and the SACP. It has also striven to project itself as a custodian of true ANC values, even though no objective basis exists for this role. The ANC has shown no preparedness to exercise control over the Youth League.

All three groups have, by the way they have operated in practice, imposed modes of operation that are fundamentally anti-democratic. The methods they invariably employ to advance their views have not eschewed violence, but have been characterised by flagrant intimidation of the members of the very public they purport to represent. They have operated in a way that implies the public is not entitled to differ with their policy preferences.

By asserting their autonomy and simultaneously denying the same to especially the ANC and other groups, they have diminished rather than expanded the realm of democracy. Although civil society is replete with many other groups that are anti-democratic, the essence of civil society is to expand the realm of democracy and freedom. In many societies the excesses of anti-democratic groups have been curbed by the State, which, in this respect, has acted as a guarantor against uncivil society.

By virtue of its relationship with powerful CSOs, the State in South Africa has been hemmed-in by these groups and is clearly limited to act against them. When they have embarked on actions that have clearly not conceded that others are entitled to views that may be opposed to those they hold, the State has looked the other way or offered limp-wristed responses that do not curb what clearly severely limits the realm of freedom.

Ineffectual crime control may have something to do with this. It not unreasonable to conclude that those who enforce the law are confused by the selective basis on which the State expects them to perform their duties. As a result, they err on the side of not or only partially enforcing the law. Criminals are clearly exploiting this confusion and, in the process, conditions for civil society to function optimally are destroyed. The ANC is effectively denied the space to appeal to all constituencies. It has lavishly followed the leadership of the SACP in espousing the cause of the working class and the poor, and at least neglected or subsumed the needs of the middle classes. Nothing should make the ANC disinclined to consider the needs of the middle classes[2] other than to attempt to please its alliance partners. What little the ANC does for middle classes is carefully choreographed not to displease the two alliance partners whose ideological preferences are anchored in a working-class bias.

Civil society as a whole has been impacted by the stance assumed by the two ANC alliance partners. Groups rooted in the middle classes have grown to be careful not to upset the SACP and COSATU lest they be reminded they serve the interest of the bourgeoisie and are counter-revolutionary. They often engage with policy issues on terms determined by groups that do not accept their legitimacy to articulate their fundamental viewpoints.

The readiness to use less than peaceful means in articulating their views derives in the main from their relationship with the ANC. They are confident that, whatever they do, they will not face prosecution. Striking workers have assaulted their non-participating colleagues and destroyed property in defiance of laws, but no attempt has been made to prosecute them. Members of especially COSATU brazenly break laws with a complete sense of impunity. Their relationship with the ANC shields them from prosecution.

It is this inability to apply the law against members of the alliance that has reduced law enforcement to a complete joke. In the eyes of the public, it is as if anyone engaged in any activity with a political objective vaguely similar to the views of the ANC is beyond prosecution. So it is that, in the name of giving voice to poor constituencies, houses and motorists have been attacked, and the assailants have not had to answer for their actions in court.

The Black Management Forum (BMF) is an organisation whose *raison d'être* is supporting the interests of management, which includes wealth accumulation. It is inconceivable that this organisation goes along with

2   Mandela, N. 1995. *Long Walk to Freedom* Little Brown& Co, p 510

the manner in which the ANC focuses on issues of poverty and workers almost to the exclusion of explicit support for measures geared towards the middle classes, especially sections seeking to accumulate wealth. While the ANC has supported measures to include black managers in businesses run by whites, this is not what all aspirant black bourgeoisie desire.

Emerging black managers, who own businesses and have little interest in working as managers in white-owned enterprises, are evident throughout the country. Managers in these businesses must be alarmed by the wage increases of almost twice the rate of inflation that COSATU unions have been demanding. Like their peers anywhere in the world, they surely must be keen to reduce costs in order to increase their businesses' profitability.

In all likelihood, such managers do not support measures advanced by COSATU that workers should be difficult to fire. Any manager wants the flexibility to reduce costs, a key component of which are labour costs, when the business cycle turns downwards. Managers know that they are not in control of the business cycle and they all want to be able to preserve their balance sheets when the cycle so demands.

COSATU, which has established tight control over the ANC,[3] has virtually forced the latter into agreeing to protect workers irrespective of economic circumstances. Whatever the business cycle, workers – especially COSATU members – must not be fired; they should retain their jobs even in a deep recession such as the economy is currently experiencing.

By allowing itself to be hauled out and paraded as supporting the ANC when convenient,[4] it is difficult to escape the conclusion that the BMF has settled into an obsequious position in its relations with the ANC. In return, they appear satisfied the ANC will retain Black Economic Empowerment (BEE) and affirmative action, as if these policies are the ultimate for all black managers. The deal between the ANC and the BMF appears to be that, for as long as the ANC creates a basis for black groups seeking to accumulate wealth using BEE laws to do so, this group will support the ANC in its endeavours to become a dominant electoral force. While there is nothing wrong with this objective, this method of accumulating capital does not define the manner in which all blacks are approaching

3   Cosatu denies it controls the ANC. See 'We do not control Zuma – Vavi' *Business Day* 17 July 2009
4   See 'Mzantsi Stars Say Together We Can Do More' undated ANC pamphlet inserted in national newspaper before the 2009 national elections.

this question. Many have preferred to assume risk, rendering affirmative action and BEE of limited use.

A useful approach that the BMF might consider, which has a greater likelihood to advance the interest of civil society, is for it to seek inclusion into the alliance on the same basis as COSATU and others. Alternatively, they should seek to be viewed as a business league in the same way that there is a women's league and a youth league. For this latter option to be considered, all members of the BMF would first have to be members of the ANC. BMF leaders should not have a problem with this, but some members may, in which case a neater option would be to form part of the alliance. The BMF is, after all, as much a distinct constituency as the youth and women's leagues, and there is no reason why there cannot be a business league within the ANC to afford this constituency a platform to contribute to the evolution of policy as do other subsidiary organisations. The BMF would certainly be better that the South African National Civic Organisation (SANCO), which, for all intents and purposes, is treated as if it were an alliance partner even though its existence as an organised force in communities is not apparent. The BMF has a membership capable of being audited. The Umkhonto we Sizwe Veterans Association (MKVA), an organisation representing former guerrillas of the ANC, has been granted status akin to an ANC subsidiary organisation. It must therefore be possible for the BMF or some such group to be admitted as a business league. This would resolve what is presently a one-way bet: the SACP and COSATU have unassailable pole-position status within the alliance that has been used to virtually take ownership of the ANC.

Other CSOs such as the taxi associations, which have obvious business interests, have used methods of struggle perfected by COSATU and the Youth League that are threatening and at times outright injurious to members of the public. Striking members of COSATU are distinguishable by the assortment of weapons they routinely bear at marches in support of their demands. These weapons have been used with deadly consequences on members of the public and those who hold a different viewpoint. Opposing a strike in a plant in which COSATU has a majority is risking not just expressing a different point of view, but also life. In some cases no questions have been asked whether individuals not engaging in strike action are members of the union. They have been attacked, at times in the presence of police officers. Truck drivers at work have simply been hauled out of their trucks and savagely assaulted for not supporting a strike. Security guards who preferred to work when their colleagues were on strike lost their lives for daring to hold different viewpoints and acting on them.

Taxi associations have put forward ridiculous demands and threatened violence in support of these demands. When on strike, they too embark on actions that make it impossible for members of the public to use public amenities such as roads.

So widespread has the violent mode of protest become, that it has been embraced as a method of choice by community groups that are upset by poor municipal service delivery.[5] When their actions are underway it is now well known that members of the public not participating in the action cannot use roads, which routinely get blockaded, and stones are hurled at motorists who do dare to use them. Why members of the public should be targeted in this way is never explained. Government also does nothing to ensure the public is able to use facilities without harm.

Such methods of struggle are profoundly anti-democratic and should be stopped by government, which should guarantee every citizen's right to hold a different view. Civil society suffers immensely from such actions. It cannot express itself fully unless freedom to do so is not in any way limited either by the State or non-State actors.

Service delivery

Service delivery protests have sprouted all over the country. They have been experienced in townships without any known organisation leading the community. There is a high degree of voluntarism in them and they tend to attract the participation of people too young to have good reason to be concerned with service delivery issues. One possible explanation for the protests is that these groups mimic the mode of protest employed by COSATU in its activities, especially strikes.

---

5   Malefane, M. & Khupiso, V. 'Angry mob disrupts Ivory Park charity work' *Sunday Times* 19 July 2009; Omarjee, H. 'ANC puts local government to the test' *Business Day* 21 July 2009

A standard explanation nevertheless for the protests has been that they are aimed at the poor record of delivery.[6] Even within government it has become conventional wisdom to understand protests that are invariably violent as symptomatic of the failure of municipalities to deliver services effectively and efficiently. This view has persisted even as protests flared up literally a few weeks after many of those involved in them voted for the current government. Surely they too must understand it takes time for a new administration to organise itself sufficiently to attend even to urgent issues. Moreover, the new administration started in office at a time the country was reeling from a contracted economy. Again many of the constituencies must have had some understanding that the ability of government to increase investment in meeting their expectations was limited by unanticipated economic difficulties.

However, there is another explanation for the by now ubiquitous protests, namely that they are a cry by marginalised communities to be included in political decision-making that plans what and how to deliver to poor communities. This explanation is plausible chiefly because it makes it understandable why people would vote a government into office and then literally a few days later mount protests against it.

Nothing government has done or said suggests a process of inclusion will be undertaken. Rather it is focused on delivering the services it thinks the people require. This displays a profound misunderstanding of the need for inclusion of groups that historically have had things done for them and has an impact on sharing power with civil society. A healthy civil society needs a government that understands that it has to surrender some of its power to CSOs.

Centralisation and civil society

Another distortive factor in the way of civil society is the centralist impulses evident in the ANC. These impulses benefit from voting patterns that have secured the position of the ANC as a dominant electoral force. Centralisation and civil society are mutually exclusive; one cannot exist alongside the other.

6   Omarjee, H. 'Zuma tells protestors state will enforce law' *Business Day* 23 July 2009

For a long time now, the ANC has fought for a united South Africa. In this, the party has sought to argue against balkanisation of the country and the federal tendencies embedded in the Bantustan system. Views that a federal form of State is well suited to the country's diverse population are well known and have provided a basis for the ANC's centralisation leanings. Adherents to federalism in South Africa have not always embraced democracy and have provided support for centralisation. The ANC has been correct to oppose this as it was not mainly advanced to enhance but to impede democracy.

Voters have also lent their support to the ANC, thus strengthening the hold of the party on power. In turn, this support has increased the impulses of the party towards centralising power. It is not incorrect to argue that the tendency to centralise within the ANC has proceeded with the knowledge of and, to a degree, the support of voters. This is, therefore, centralisation of a democratic variety.

However correct the ANC has been in its leanings towards centralisation, the fact remains that centralisation is inimical to democracy and a thriving civil society. Even parties that centralise with the consent of voters create conditions unfavourable for the expansion of civil society.

Civil society and the decentralisation of political power have a long and happy history together. Its birthmarks clearly reveal that it emerged from struggles against centralisation of political power[7] and has since thrived in environments of decentralised power. Early church-dominated Europe gave rise to civil society that opposed both papal and royal dominance. Early civil society sought to diversify power so that constituencies outside of government could also be repositories of power. Once the idea that the State and church should be separate had been accepted, it was easy for royalty to accept co-governance with individuals who had risen to power in emerging towns and burgeoning tradesmen.

The idea of a law-governed society emerged not just to curb the power of the sovereign, but also that of civil society.[8] Institutions created to limit the power of the State in South Africa are often viewed as usurping its policy-making role. On more than one occasion the courts have been accused of confusing their judicial role with a policy-making role that belongs exclusively to government. While the boundary between the role

7 Hall, JA. 1995. 'In Search of Civil Society' *Civil Society: Theory, History, Comparison* Wiley, p 7
8 Hall, JA. *op. cit.* pp 5-6

of the courts in testing especially the constitutionality of legislation and policy-making is very thin, it would help democracy for policy-makers to err on the side of yielding to the courts. This would enhance democracy by underscoring the fact that government too should be accountable to people and institutions other than those who voted it into office.

In societies marked by power situated in diverse locations, the only glue that could hold the society together was a set of commonly agreed rules to regulate the behaviour of all with power.[9] This idea evolved into parliaments to represent the population. Each stage of the evolution of representation of people with power is marked by failure and success. Its high point, though, is the depersonalisation of power.

Centralisation impulses in the governing party are at odds with the idea of diversified power. Note should be taken that the argument made here is not that the governing party is leaning towards centralisation with a view to deliberately limiting democracy. The major objective, government argues, is to advance development – an objective likely to strike a chord with many groups as many people accept that development is necessary and urgent. The levels of poverty and marginalisation are so high that development to erode these will in all likelihood be welcomed by many people.

Many societies, however, have become less democratic than desirable because governments successfully drew a distinction between development and democracy and proceeded as if these were mutually exclusive. They are not mutually exclusive; they can proceed simultaneously and, if allowed to, can be self-reinforcing. India is a country that has succeeded in implementing development while simultaneously building democracy, and the outcome is there for all to see.

In South Africa, the development-first argument takes the form of eliminating or severely limiting the powers of provinces. Provinces are viewed as standing in the way of effecting development and it has been suggested that their powers be curtailed to allow for the centre to implement development without opposition. Embedded in this is a process that will inevitably lead to undemocratic outcomes, which, in turn, will have injurious consequences for civil society. Centralised political arrangements, even in modern times, are inconsistent with a flourishing civil

9 Hall, JA. *op. cit.* pp 3-7

society. In the case of South Africa, a civil society already under strain imposed by the domineering role of COSATU and its allies, centralisation will have an even greater deleterious effect.

A Disguised Opportunity?

Political Fluidity, Civil Society and Democracy

Steven Friedman
Centre for the Study of Democracy
Rhodes University/University of
Johannesburg

Has 18 months of political turmoil opened or closed opportunities for civil society? The defeat of former President Mbeki at the African National Congress (ANC) conference in Polokwane in late 2007, and Jacob Zuma's ascendancy to the presidency, have important implications for civil society organisations (CSOs), but there is no agreement on what these are. The changes have opened three lines of analysis, each with different implications for CSOs. The first sees the changes as a threat to the limited influence that civil society has enjoyed since 1994. In this view, the new leadership is far more interested in placing its stamp on society than listening to independent voices; CSOs that do not enjoy links with the ANC leadership are likely to be banished even further into the wilderness than they have over the past decade. The second view is almost a polar opposite. It sees the new ANC leadership as a rebellion against centralised, 'top down' leadership, which stilled those voices it would rather not hear. The challenge to former President Mbeki has, it is argued, freed not only the ANC, but also society from the dead hand of direction from the top. The result must be the removal of the constraints that stifled debate, which will open new opportunities for CSOs to express themselves and influence government decisions. The third view is sceptical of the intentions of the new leadership and that which it replaced. But it argues that the changes must open new spaces for civil society influence because the fluidity they have introduced means that the new government leadership is not united and has no agreed vision for the future. In this context, it is argued, decision-makers are more likely to take civil society seriously: divisions within the ANC mean that they will be searching for allies, and the fluidity means they may be looking for solutions to governance problems.

This chapter will examine the impact of current political changes on civil society using a recent exercise conducted by the Centre for the Study of Democracy in which CSOs – including Idasa – were invited to discuss the political environment and its implications. It will report the view of CSOs and then offer its own interpretation. Before that, some comments on the state of civil society in South Africa are necessary.

The state of civil society

Civil society has come to be seen as a realm of virtue across the political spectrum. It can be regarded as a desirable force by conservatives seeking to limit the State's role in meeting citizens' welfare needs[1] and by left-wingers who see it as the most effective available field of grassroots action against privilege.[2] It is seen by some as a realm in which citizens escape the reach of majority government, and by others as the means by which the majority claim the decision-making rights to which democracy entitles them. The approach adopted here is to see civil society as a realm in which citizens acquire a voice, enabling them to ensure that government responds to their needs and is accountable to them. This requires that citizens enjoy independent access to the means to organise, which, in turn, is only possible if those who wish to organise enjoy access to resources that are not generated by the State. Civil society is not open only to those whose values we share, but to all citizens. This point needs stressing because, in South Africa over the past two decades, the term 'civil society' has been used to describe only those organisations of which

1   Tanner, M. 1996. *The End of Welfare: Fighting Poverty in the Civil Society* Washington DC, Cato Institute
2   Keane, J. 1988. *Democracy and Civil Society* London, Verso; Keane, J. (ed.) 1998. *Civil Society and the State* London, Verso

the speaker approves. However, if we understand civil society as the realm of citizen voice and acknowledge that democratic principle requires that all enjoy a say, the test of democracy's health is not whether our favoured section of civil society is able to participate, but whether all can. A look at the current state of South African civil society suggests that many voices are indeed excluded. For those able to participate in it, civil society remains vigorous and effective, but there is strong evidence that civil society is shallow because many people do not enjoy access to it. Participation in civil society requires resources, including the ability to gain access to government institutions. Successive studies have found that the poor continue to remain outside civil society, ensuring that CSOs that champion the poor have weak roots among them. This is best illustrated by clear evidence that the voicelessness of the poor hampers democracy's ability to respond to poverty. Repeatedly, research shows that the development debate ignores the wishes and needs of poor people because the poor are not organised into associations that could ensure their voice is heard between elections.

The poor do organise and act collectively, but, because collective action by poor people is led by organisations unwilling or unable to participate in the national policy debate, it is unable to impact on priorities. A key example is the wave of grassroots protest since 2005. The concerns and demands of protesters are usually muffled or obliterated entirely by commentary and reportage that explains away demonstrations by labelling them 'service delivery protests' – a practice that is anti-democratic in two ways: first, because it silences the protesters by substituting an elite-generated explanation of their actions for an attempt to investigate and listen to their grievances, and because it assumes, inaccurately, that people at the grassroots are passive recipients of government 'delivery', rather than choosing and thinking citizens who demand a part in the discussion on the way in which government is to serve them.[3]

Research has found significant grassroots activity by the poor, but most of it is devoted to activities designed to secure 'collective sustenance' – 'survivalist' mutual aid activities, rather than advocacy for policy change. A key challenge for civil society activities seeking to enhance the representation of the poor may, therefore, be to secure stronger linkages between the grassroots 'survivalist' groups on the one hand and CSOs, government institutions, media, and policy and strategy specialists on the other.[4] Until that happens, the advocates of policy change will remain cut off from the poor, while the organisations of the poor remain cut off from the policy debate.

In summary, claims that civil society has been inactive since 1994 are not supported by the evidence: CSOs have participated in the national debate frequently and often effectively. But many, probably most, citizens have remained outside civil society. What difference, if any, have political events made to this diagnosis?

Hard times for civil society?

If a series of discussions with CSOs over the past few months[5] is a guide, the organisations expect more difficult times ahead – not new possibilities.

The discussions held in 2009 brought together organisations, most of whom were firmly part of that section of civil society which works for an extension of rights and for greater social equity. Organisations working on gender issues were particularly prominent. Not all were part of this camp; participation was also sought by 'apolitical' organisations and by two seeking to speak for white Afrikaners. Much of the analysis presented here will be misleading unless it is understood that the dominant perspective was that of 'progressive' organisations seeking a more inclusive and equitable society.

In the view of most organisations, but particularly those pressing for greater expansion of human rights on issues such as gender and sexual preference, the changes held far more threat than promise. First, they detected a change in the rhetoric of ruling party politicians on issues such as sexual preference. Remarks by the president were cited as evidence and the fact that they were later retracted was not seen as significant. This, it was suggested, was but one example of an environment in which rights that seemed fairly entrenched before 2008 – at least in principle – were under threat. Another example, it was argued, was a more hostile attitude

---

4   Centre for Policy Studies, Civil Society and Poverty Reduction in Southern Africa, JHB, CPS, mimeo, July 2002
    'Civil Society and Poverty Reduction'
5   McKaiser, E. June 2009. 'Session One – Summary of Main Threads' Notes prepared for Centre for the Study of
    Democracy Discussion

towards the rights of accused persons, who were sometimes portrayed by politicians as an obstacle to the fight against crime.[6] It was argued that political change had enabled sections of the new ANC leadership to express socially conservative views that were previously taboo in government. This would clearly weaken the influence of human rights activism. A further source of pessimism was the claim that political pressure was being placed on oversight bodies, including institutions such as the Human Rights Commission, which was threatened with budget cuts if, for example, it was to try to hold ANC politicians to account.[7] While this remains a claim only, it illustrates a very high level of apprehension.

Second, it was argued that ruling party politicians were now far more inclined to value party loyalty. This had two consequences: greater intolerance of or the propensity to ignore groups and individuals who were not considered loyal to the ruling party, and a greater tendency to rely on the ANC and its members, rather than citizens organised independently in civil society, to debate and resolve issues. Civil society influence was, therefore, more difficult to wield and increasingly dependant on loyalty to the ruling party. Greater emphasis on party loyalty was also bound, activists noted, to affect relations between CSOs and the dynamics within them. Because civil society is inevitably ideologically and politically diverse, it is divided along several axes, including support for and opposition to the ANC. A stress on party loyalty was likely to create tensions between organisations sympathetic to the governing party and those independent or critical of it. And, the closer an organisation was to the governing party, the more likely pressure would be exerted within it to ensure loyalty to the ANC leadership. This second point is important if it is recalled that civil society is a realm in which citizens express voice within the organisations they join as well as to political power-holders. Suppressing voices within CSOs is, therefore, a significant diminution of democracy. The extent to which this practice threatens democracy obviously depends on how large and influential the organisation is.

Third, fears were expressed that, although politicians in power made 'the right consultative noises',[8] spaces for civil society influence were not

---

6   'Shabangu grilled on "shoot-to-kill" remarks' Independent Online 10 April 2008 http://www.iol.co.za/index. php?set_id=1&click_id=6&art_id=nw20080410173651309C804202
7   McKaiser, E. July 2009. 'Summary of Session Two: Civil Society Round Table Discussions' Notes prepared for Centre for the Study of Democracy Discussion
8   McKaiser, June 2009

opening up. The encouraging statements might, therefore, prove to be electoral posturing. As a consequence, even where CSOs can engage with government on policy, they have little or no impact on the ensuing decisions. Activists engaged in pressing for change on, for example, gender violence and land reform, described participating in policy processes that produced no real change in policy or government practice. At most it was suggested the new political leadership spoke the language of engagement and listening while acting differently. Government decisions, in this view, remain at least as immune to influence as they were under the old ANC leadership.

These views were not unanimous, but they were dominant – particularly among groups concerned to deepen and broaden human rights and those fighting for greater social equity. They are based on evidence: politicians did indeed make the statements that are worrying a section of civil society, and the judgment that there is no greater opportunity for civil society to influence decisions is clearly based on real experiences. Nevertheless, there appears to be good reason to rethink the claim that opportunities for civil society influence – and, therefore, for an important dimension of citizen voice – are narrowing.

Strategic perspectives

Part of the critique discussed here may exaggerate the constraints facing civil society.

First, it is possible that some of the 'new' trends identified by CSOs are aspects of an environment with which civil society has been living for some time. The complaint that government is no more willing to listen to civil society now obviously acknowledges, by implication, that it was not particularly willing to listen before. While participants were able to cite convincing evidence that government was talking to them but not listening, few offered evidence that its willingness to listen had diminished.

While there have been recent attacks on rights, this does not mean that support for these attacks is unanimous. There was substantial support for the view that there was considerable disunity in government and the ANC.[9] A participant suggested that, while social conservatism prevails among political leadership, 'there is ideological fluidity within the State, making it difficult to accurately gauge the issue'.[10] If there is both unity and fluidity, it follows logically that the stated positions that concern rights-based civil society campaigners are contested within the ANC and government. Thus, while Jacob Zuma did make statements about gays during 2008, when he was president of the ANC, which indicated deep intolerance, he was obliged to apologise, presumably in response to pressure within the ANC.[11] The greater prevalence of anti-rights rhetoric now may mean only that differences that existed within the ANC alliance over the past decade, but which were suppressed, are being aired – not that the social conservatives now rule. The dominant pattern seems to be internal contest, suggesting that rights-based campaigners may have allies as well as opponents within the ANC and government.

While apprehension about attacks on rights are understandable – South Africa has no rights tradition and the protection offered by the Constitution is fragile in a divided society with wide inequalities – the evidence suggests that they do not accurately describe the strategic environment facing CSOs since they do not recognise opportunities and threats. While the constraints are real, the greatest opportunity for civil society influence is the division within political leadership and the fluidity mentioned earlier. As long as government decision-makers have differing values and interests, and as long as there is no rigid ideological consensus among the governing elite, CSOs must enjoy the potential to win allies among political leaders and to use these as a source of influence.[12] Providing there are senior politicians who remain sympathetic to rights, the fact that some of their colleagues are hostile to them need not prevent CSOs from advancing closer to their goals.

Evidence that CSOs can, provided they identify the issues on which government may be willing to listen and use their resources strategically, wield influence even in seemingly hostile environments is provided by

9 McKaiser, *op. cit.*
10 McKaiser, July 2009
11 'Zuma sorry for "gay" remarks' *News24* 26 September 2008 http://www.news24.com/News24/South_Africa/Zuma/0,,2-7-1840_2005231,00.html
12 Throughout the conflict between government and the Treatment Action Campaign, the TAC actively sought and received the support of allies in government whose intervention – or, indeed their refusal to intervene to enforce government decisions – played an important role in creating space for responses that served the needs of people living with HIV/AIDS.

one of the least likely stories of post-1994 civil society: the success of organisations drawn from the white right. The trade union Solidarity and the activist alliance AfriForum, both born of the white trade union movement and, more specifically, opposition to affirmative action, seem highly implausible candidates for influence with an ANC government committed to racial change. Yet both have perhaps exercised at least as much influence as CSOs close to the ruling party. During discussions, they were far more optimistic about the prospects of working with government than any other organisation.[13] There are obvious limits to the influence of groups representing white interests, whose key goal is to end or substantially reduce the impact of affirmative action, and they are not about to persuade government to abandon its commitment to use positive measures to attack inherited racial inequality. But their strength appears to lie in their recognition that this need not prevent them from winning gains on issues that do not challenge core government policy. They have particularly flourished since Zuma took over the ANC, and have benefited from a coincidence of effective strategy and the realisation that the new ANC leadership wants to repair some of the damage it believes the Mbeki administration inflicted on race relations. It seems reasonable to assume that CSOs far closer to the ruling party's stated values could win similar influence if they too focused on the strategically possible.

At least part of the current constraints on civil society influence may, therefore, lie in a failure to read the strategic environment and to develop effective responses to it. A greater willingness to think strategically about opportunities and constraints would enhance civil society influence. A more general criticism is that the approach adopts a too restrictive view of civil society's prospects by focusing excessively on direct contact with government and on the attitudes of its leadership.

Looking beyond government

Engagement with government is an essential feature of civil society activity. This does not mean, however, that civil society can only engage if government wants it to do so. CSOs in many societies have an important

---

13 McKaiser, June 2009

role in pressing governments to become more open to citizen voice, despite the fact that this was not initially what governments had in mind. Much of the debate among civil society activists discussed in this book seems to assume that effective citizenship relies on direct engagement with government to influence policy processes. This is illustrated, for example, by a preoccupation with the statements of government leaders, the workings of formal policy processes, and the outcomes of direct interaction between activists and government leaders. If that were so, activists would be entirely correct to insist that, unless government is willing to welcome them and their concerns into the policy debate, they are deprived of influence. However, CSOs can influence events without talking to anyone in government for long periods, and in contexts in which government is explicitly excluding them from official policy processes. The Treatment Action Campaign (TAC) won the adoption by government of a comprehensive AIDS plan and substantial changes in government practice during a period in which it was excluded from the official policy forum: the South African National AIDS Council (SANAC).[14] The Basic Income Grant campaign has probably helped to expand the reach of social grants, despite operating in an environment in which government made it clear that its demands would not be met.[15]

If civil society success does not depend solely on direct engagement with government, it is inappropriate to assess strategic possibilities purely through an analysis concerned only with whether government will endorse civil society positions and work with activists to translate them into law or programmes. It is, rather, necessary to examine the social context to establish whether it opens opportunities for influence regardless of government's attitude. The TAC strategy was based partly on building 'moral consensus' within society, which was meant to change government's position simply because the weight of moral pressure from society would become too great. A related strategic goal was to build alliances, which would turn that moral consensus into purposive action.[16] This approach was based on the key assumption that government is forced to respond to society, however much it may try to insulate itself, and that, if government

14 Friedman and Mottiar 'A Rewarding Engagement? The Treatment Action Campaign and the Politics of HIV/AIDS', Politics and Society 2005 no 33 pp 511–565
15 Coleman, N. 2003. *Current Debates Around BIG: The Political and Socio-Economic Context* Development Policy Research Unit, University of CapeTown
16 Friedman and Mottiar 'A Rewarding Engagement?'

is not sympathetic to a goal, society may be better disposed to it and organised enough to exert influence. In some cases even public consensus in government can be an advantage, since it may trigger resistance within society that could turn implacable government attitudes into opportunities rather than obstacles. The government approach to AIDS under President Mbeki is an obvious example and it is surely no coincidence that one of the key campaigns in which an influential social coalition challenged government was prompted by its approach to HIV/AIDS.

An approach built on this insight would still need to know about decision-making trends within government. But it would also need to know about strategic alignments within society to understand which social groups may be allies and which opponents. Who in society may rally behind a demand, in what circumstances and with what implications is, therefore, as important a question as who in government supports or opposes a call for change. It is this realisation that, no doubt, prompted the argument that strategic possibilities for effective voice did exist, even as it decried government's response to demands.[17]

Direct engagement with government is a key determinant of civil society influence, but hardly the only one. It may also be more accurate to see effective direct engagement with government as a consequence, not a cause, of influence. CSOs are likely to enjoy influence over government policy either because they are close to government or because they have mobilised enough influence in society to force the authorities to listen. Since most lack the former advantage, the limits and possibilities of influence in the current context will be shaped as much, if not more, by the degree to which they can build influence in society through strategic alliances than whether government wants to talk to them. The social environment in which organisations operate is a far more important test of influence than the goodwill of people in government.

It is here that the shallowness of civil society becomes a key strategic constraint. While influence does not depend only on the number of citizens on whose behalf organisations speak, organisations that can mobilise a substantial constituency are likely to exert more influence than those that cannot. This analysis has implied that the government claim – in this society and others – that civil society has no right to tell the authorities what to do because government is elected and therefore speaks for society,[18] ignores the reality that being elected does not automatically equip politicians to know what their electors want on particular policy issues.[19] However, if we understand civil society as a realm in which citizens acquire voice, it should follow that those who speak for more people have a greater right to be heard. Particularly where organisations purport to speak for the concerns of people at the grassroots, the claim is more likely to be taken seriously if the organisations directly represent those on whose behalf they speak.

Civil society influence today is hardly guaranteed, particularly for organisations not allied to the ruling party. But the current climate appears more open to influence than the pessimism of most organisations suggests – if we understand influence as a capacity built in society and recognise that government attitudes are only one among several strategic issues that CSOs need to take into account. To see it as the only one is to miss the opportunities a democratic system offers.

The rules rule: Centrality of constitutional democracy

The preceding analysis has assumed that constitutional democracy will remain in place; without it, civil society cannot organise or seek support.

There can be no civil society without democracy. Implicit in the analysis proposed here is that CSOs use the rights guaranteed by democracy to acquire voice on behalf of citizens. Democratic rules are, therefore, the essential precondition for all civil society activity. Clearly, none of the courses of action proposed for CSOs in this analysis, such as mobilising public opinion and actively seeking allies in society, would be possible unless democratic rules remain in force.

This suggests that the key issue facing CSOs in the current political environment is not whether government officials are sympathetic to their concerns, but whether the rules of constitutional democracy will remain in place, protecting their right to campaign and organise. The discussions

18 Centre for the Study of Democracy 'Session Three Notes'
19 Riker, W. & Ordeshook, P. 1968. 'A theory of the calculus of voting' *American Political Science Review*, 62:25-42

showed that there is some recognition of this among civil society activists – thus part of the discussion revolved around a proposed amendment to the Constitution that would allow parliament, in effect, to override the Constitution to protect government from paying in full citizens who launch successful claims against it.[20] A key concern was that this would narrow the rights available to citizens and may, therefore, inhibit civil society activity. But it is not at all clear that civil society activists are as concerned about attacks on the right to speak and organise as they are about the specific rights for which they campaign. If civil society is to flourish in this environment, it is essential that its activists realise that the most important rights in the Constitution for those who seek a rights-based order are not those protecting the specific rights of particular social groups (such as women, gays and lesbians), or those seeking to entrench equity by enforcing social and economic rights, but those protecting the right to participate fully in the national debate – if necessary, by mobilising citizens. However sympathetic some in government or the courts may seem to specific rights, these rights will not endure if they are not defended. 'First generation rights' protecting the right to act and speak are essential if that defence is to be possible. If CSOs recognise that reliance on contact with government will need to be supplemented by active citizenship for them to wield influence, the preservation and strengthening of the measures that make this possible will need to be a key concern for civil society.

Two aspects of this task need highlighting. First, while the right to act and speak of those who are connected enough to participate in the mainstream national debate has been protected by constitutional democracy since 1994, there is substantial evidence that social movements have been subject to harassment.[21] National politicians may have no role in this assault on the right to mobilise and organise, but it is central to civil society activity and has received little attention from the national debate. The only CSOs that have expressed concern are the social movements themselves. If CSOs attempt to deepen their roots in society and to connect with the grassroots, the right to act on the ground will become crucial. The more political office holders are persuaded to insist that local

20 Centre for the Study of Democracy 'Session Three Notes'
21 Western Cape Anti-Eviction Campaign Press Alert: Mzonke Poni to appear in the Somerset West Court and various similar posts. http://www.ukzn.ac.za/ccs

leaders allow others to campaign in their areas, the greater civil society influence is likely to be. Achieving free activity in the townships and shack settlements is thus a core civil society strategic goal.

Political turmoil has also placed pressure on key democratic institutions such as the judiciary, the media and universities. ANC leaders, prompted by President Zuma's legal difficulties, accused judges of being 'counter revolutionary' or being hostile to democracy if they were seen to be unsympathetic to Zuma.[22] Immediately after the decision by national prosecutors to withdraw charges against Zuma, South African Communist Party (SACP) general secretary (now Minister of Higher Education) Blade Nzimande insisted on action to reform the judiciary, although he said he wanted to strengthen judicial independence. South Africa has a long history of politicians claiming to extend freedoms when they plan the opposite – for example, universities were strictly segregated by the Extension of *University* Education Act (1959) – and Nzimande's demand was seen by his critics as an attempt to control the courts. When Zuma used the same language in his State of the Nation address some weeks after the election, it prompted predictable anxiety. This concern is heightened by the reality that it is possible to undermine checks on government without changing the Constitution, simply by appointing to key posts people sympathetic to political power holders. The ANC has also called for a media tribunal and ANC leaders, including Zuma, have complained about what they see as members of the public's limited ability to seek redress from newspapers who treat them unfairly. Academic freedom may have been threatened by the demand of ANC-aligned youth organisations that the head of the University of South Africa (UNISA), Barney Pityana, be removed,[23] although Nzimande did assure Pityana that his job was safe.

These developments have, again, received little attention from much of civil society – perhaps because they appear to be disputes between politicians, with little relevance for organisations. However, an independent judiciary, a free media and academics willing to follow the argument wherever it leads remain crucial to the democratic environment that civil society needs. Without them, civil society would find it very difficult to act effectively. The principled protection of democratic institutions is critical

22 Mohau Pheko 'If you must insult judges, Mr Mantashe, raise your standard of propaganda' *Sunday Times* 19 July 2008
23 'Pityana Must Go. He is running UNISA like a spaza shop – Ngobese' *Sowetan* 18 May 2009

to civil society's future and may, therefore, need to become a key strategic concern of all civil society. This is a factor that unites organisations across other barriers as an issue of common concern because, as this analysis argued earlier, civil society is free only if all organisations are free.

The task for much of civil society is to move beyond a reliance on direct engagement with government to a strategy that stresses more the need to deepen roots in society. Preserving the freedoms that make this possible is a core concern. Civil society's immediate future may thus depend on how energetically and effectively it unites behind the institutions and rights that make civil society possible. If democracy is preserved, civil society's possibilities may be greater than its organisations and activists currently think. If it is not, civil society's prospects will be bleak. As always, civil society and democracy feed off each other.

www.ingramcontent.com/pod-product-compliance
Lightning Source LLC
Chambersburg PA
CBHW030657270326
41929CB00007B/409